Early Praise for *C Brain Teasers*

I first encountered C as a computer science major at The University of
Florida, where I learned enough to use it for my senior project, and found
it much more interesting than, say, COBOL. I've since programmed profes-
sionally in everything from IBM/370 assembler to Java and Python—and,
briefly, COBOL—but I've never forgotten the delight I took in that project.
Working through this collection of brain teasers has brought that all back
for me. I don't expect to write much C any time soon, but I always enjoy
getting in touch with my roots, and being reminded of a time when I couldn't
take things like memory allocation and garbage collection for granted. I hope
you will enjoy this book as much as I have.

➤ **David Rupp**
Senior Software Development Engineer, IMDb

Programming in C can be a brain teaser in itself, so it's nice to have Dan
Gookin's book as a place to practice our skills. It's a guided tour through
many of C's tricky spots, with explanations of the hazard and how to avoid
it in your code. Some C-based math puzzles round things out, so it's not all
traps and tricks.

➤ **Andy Lester**
Author, *Land the Tech Job You Love*

This short book covers a lot of meaningful topics for a C programmer. It
explains some common pitfalls and misunderstandings with concise and
easy-to-read examples that show why you should or shouldn't do something,
along with showing some interesting algorithms.

➤ **Nick McGinness**
Staff Software Engineer, Direct Supply

C Brain Teasers

Exercise Your Mind

Dan Gookin

The Pragmatic Bookshelf

Dallas, Texas

When we are aware that a term used in this book is claimed as a trademark, the designation is printed with an initial capital letter or in all capitals.

The Pragmatic Starter Kit, The Pragmatic Programmer, Pragmatic Programming, Pragmatic Bookshelf, PragProg and the linking *g* device are trademarks of The Pragmatic Programmers, LLC.

Every precaution was taken in the preparation of this book. However, the publisher assumes no responsibility for errors or omissions, or for damages that may result from the use of information (including program listings) contained herein.

For our complete catalog of hands-on, practical, and Pragmatic content for software developers, please visit *https://pragprog.com*.

The team that produced this book includes:

Publisher:	Dave Thomas
COO:	Janet Furlow
Executive Editor:	Susannah Davidson
Series Editor:	Miki Tebeka
Development Editor:	Don N. Hagist
Copy Editor:	Karen Galle
Layout:	Gilson Graphics

For sales, volume licensing, and support, please contact *support@pragprog.com*.

For international rights, please contact *rights@pragprog.com*.

ISBN-13: 979-8-88865-048-6
Book version: P1.0—March 2024

Contents

Preface

Shocking all the experts who continue to predict its demise, the C Programming language is stronger than ever. Taught in universities and used by developers around the world, C's syntax and structure are borrowed by other major languages. Often, those languages have their foundation in C. Today, C is used to maintain operating systems, create high-end graphics drivers, program microcontrollers, code for embedded systems, and more.

In this book, you'll find 25 puzzles that explore the potential and possibilities of the C language. These puzzles range from easy tasks to the complex and tricky. Some puzzles showcase how limited C can be—and how to get around these limitations. The goal is to showcase various aspects of C and programming in general.

C programmers, from beginners to advanced, will gain understanding from the puzzles presented in this book. Whether you're just starting out or have been coding for a while, the insights and surprises offered here will entertain and delight you. The goal is to make you a better programmer.

How to Use This Book

This book contains 25 programming puzzles. Some perform specific tasks, while others may attempt to do something that doesn't quite work. All of the code is written in C and adheres to the C11 standard. No additional files or libraries are required. The programs run in the text mode environment, specifically, under Linux in a terminal window.

For each puzzle, your job is to guess what happens. You can predict the output, guess what the program is trying to accomplish, or identify a potential problem. The answer is revealed on the pages that follow each puzzle, along with an insight into understanding the code, what it does, and how or why it fails to do what you might think it does. The point is to learn more about C programming, witness a few tricks, and put your new knowledge to work in your own programs.

Here's a sample puzzle:

```c
int puts(const char *s);

#define lineout(a) puts(a)
#define end return(0)

int main()
{
        lineout("Hello there!");
        end;
}
```

Can you guess the output from this code? Yes, it's C source code, though I've taken some liberties with the way things are expressed. If you can guess the output, can you identify the liberties I've taken in the source code? When presented in the text, your task is to do so before you turn the page to see my explanation and further exploration of the puzzle.

Because I'm a nice guy, here are the answers:

- The output is the string "Hello there!" followed by a newline. This is the output generated by the puts() function, normally declared within the stdio.h header—but this header is missing in the source code!

- Instead of including the entire stdio.h header, I write the puts() function prototype. This is a legal move, as you can prototype any function you've created. But, here I just looked up the main page definition for puts() and copied it into my source code. Properly prototyped, the function works just fine. (Remember that the function's mechanics are stored in the library, not in the header file.)

- Two defines create the unusual statements found in the main() function. The first defines a function lineout() equivalent to the puts() function. The a in both represents the function's argument. So lineout() replaces puts() in the main() function, carrying out the same task.

- The second define assigns the return(0) statement to the word end. The result is the main() function's statements appear alien—very non-C-like. Still, the preprocessor replaces both lineout() and end with the proper C statements.

This funky construction is one of the things I adore about the C language. While as a programmer your goal should be to write easily readable text, you can add your own quirks to the language just to keep things interesting. But on a grander scale, you can use these tricks to help simplify some complex operations. So, while my attempts obfuscated the code, you can use the same tools to make a program more readable. And hopefully, you'll have fun while doing so.

Required Tools

The code presented in this book is quick and to the point. You can copy it directly from the text (type it in) or you can obtain the puzzles from my GitHub account: github.com/dangookin/C_Brain_Teasers.

All programs run in the terminal window, which is where I do my coding. I use Vim to write the source code. I build (compile and link) with clang version 14.0.0. The command line code I use to build the program is clang -Wall followed by the source code filename. This command creates the program file named a.out, which you can run by typing ./a.out at the command prompt.

The terminal window is available in Linux and on the Macintosh under macOS. For Windows, you can obtain the Linux runtime environment, which provides the same functionality. See https://learn.microsoft.com/en-us/windows/wsl/install.

To install clang in Linux, use the package manager for your distro. For example, if the distro uses apt, the command is: sudo apt-get install clang.

If you're into Integrated Development Environments (IDEs), I recommend Visual Studio Code. It's available free at https://code.visualstudio.com/.

My coding style is close to the original K&R (Kernighan and Ritchie). I use only the traditional C comments. Remember that in C, whitespace is ignored. Feel free to use your own coding style if you desire to transcribe the examples.

Remember that some of the programs do not run properly as presented. Mistakes are made on purpose to drive home a point that's explained in this text. I understand that readers who are concerned about this approach probably aren't reading this Preface, yet I write this warning anyway.

Contacting the Author

I'm happy to provide feedback or offer advice related to my C programming books. You can contact me at mailto:dgookin@wambooli.com. That's my real email address, and I try to respond to all my mail, especially specific questions regarding my books. I cannot write code for you, though I can try to help with problems you encounter related to this book.

The support page for this book can be found on my C For Dummies website at https://c-for-dummies.com/cbrainteasers. I run a blog on that site, where you can learn more about C programming with weekly lessons and monthly exercises. The site has been up for over ten years, so it covers a lot of ground. Use the search box to locate topics of interest.

Have fun solving the puzzles!

Dan Gookin, March 2024

Part I

C Brain Teasers

Count the Digits

```c
#include <stdio.h>
#include <math.h>

int main()
{
        printf("%2.4f\n", M_PI); /* M_PI = 3.14159265358979323846 */

        return(0);
}
```

Guess the Output

 Try to guess what the output is before moving to the next page.

The program displays the following output:

```
3.1416
```

Discussion

The defined constant M_PI is declared in the math.h header file. It represents the value of π out to 20 digits. Any floating point value could be specified in the printf() statement, though M_PI represents a known value with oodles of digits after the decimal.

The %2.4f placeholder directs the printf() statement to output a floating point value in a width of six digits: a minimum of two to the left of the decimal and four to the right. Because only one digit is to the left of the decimal, one character is output; a space isn't added. For the right of the decimal, only four digits are output. The value of the last digit is rounded, in this case up.

The Nerdy Details on printf() Formatting

The power in the printf() function comes from the % placeholders, which format the output. While a single conversion specifier directs printf() to output a specific format—%f for floating point, for example—more directions can dwell between the % sign and the conversion specifier to further hone the output. These specifiers define or restrict the output width.

Here are the options available for the %f placeholder:

```
%[significant][.][decimal]f
```

Two optional values, significant and decimal, set output width values left or right of the decimal, which is also optional.

Here is the output when using the %6f placeholder:

```
3.141593
```

Six digits are output after the decimal. When using the %6.f placeholder, this text is output:

```
3
```

Five spaces appear before the three. To see them, prefix the six with a zero: The %06.f placeholder outputs this text:

```
000003
```

You may find this output frustratingly inconsistent—and you're correct. It's difficult to gauge what the output will be unless you've completely immersed yourself in the features and quirks for the %f placeholder's width specifiers. Who has time for that?

A printf() Cheat You Probably Don't Know About

To better understand how many characters the printf() statement outputs, I use a common and little-known trick: the function's return value represents the number of characters in the output. Here is an update to the code:

```
#include <stdio.h>
#include <math.h>

int main()
{
        int n;

        n = printf("%2.4f\n", M_PI);
        printf("(That's %d characters)\n", n);

        return(0);
}
```

The output now looks like this:

```
3.1416
(That's 7 characters)
```

The output counts the newline, which is why 7 appears instead of 6. Also note that the output is rounded, not truncated.

The printf() function's return value, saved in variable n, provides a solid resource for the number of characters output, including the decimal (period). Alas, you can't use this printf() value until after the function returns, which means that you must approximate the number of characters output if that's a concern at runtime. Or you can use snprintf() to store the output in a buffer for further examination.

Further Reading

Detailed list of conversion specifiers and their options
    https://cplusplus.com/reference/cstdio/printf/

Placeholder/conversion specifier overview
    https://c-for-dummies.com/blog/?p=288

A Fraction of an Int

```c
#include <stdio.h>

int main()
{
        int a, b;

        a = 5; b = 4;
        printf("%d/%d = %f\n", a, b, a/b);

        return(0);
}
```

Guess the Output

Try to guess what the output is before moving to the next page.

The compiler throws a warning as the %f placeholder specifies a float value whereas integers appear as the corresponding argument.

The program displays the following output:

```
5/4 = 0.000000
```

The result, 0.000000, is accurate because dividing the integer values results in zero; int data types cannot contain fractions.

Discussion

In C programming (and many other programming languages), it's possible to divide integer values when the values divide evenly: 10/2, 8/4, 96/12, and so on. When the result contains a decimal portion, however, the computer gets all steamy and generates output like the sample code.

Several approaches are available to obtain accurate results when dividing two integer values. Of course, you can always use real numbers instead, but this approach isn't always practical. For example, if one of the variables is used in a loop, an integer is more desirable (and accurate). The common approach is to typecast the expression:

```
(float)a/b
```

The float typecast directs the program to treat int variables a and b as floating-point or real number values. This technique is known as an *explicit type conversion*. The output reflects the proper calculation:

```
5/4 = 1.250000
```

You could also specify (float)a/(float)b, though you need to only typecast the expression a/b.

If one of the values is already a real number, typecasting isn't necessary. Only when both values are integers, and they don't divide evenly, do you need to typecast.

Other Typecasting Tidbits

Beyond performing math, typecasting is used to ensure that a program's variables match the datatypes required in a function. For example, you may use integer variables in your code, but a function requires a long or unsigned integer value. To avoid the compiler getting cross with you, a typecast is used:

```
srand( (unsigned)time(NULL) );
```

I use the above statement to seed the random number generator. A clock tick value is returned from the time() function when NULL is specified as its argument, but the value may be a signed integer. To ensure a negative number isn't used as the srand() function's argument, the unsigned typecast is used.

Further Reading

Review and examples of typecasting in C
https://www.tutorialspoint.com/cprogramming/c_type_casting.htm

Explanation of implicit versus explicit type conversions
https://developerinsider.co/type-casting-c-programming/

Really good but potentially nerdy details on explicit type conversions
https://en.cppreference.com/w/cpp/language/explicit_cast

String or Not?

```
#include <stdio.h>

int main()
{
        char nonstring[] = {
                'g', 'r', 'e', 'e', 't',
                'i', 'n', 'g', 's', ',',
                ' ', 'h', 'u', 'm', 'a', 'n'
        };
        char data[] = { 127, 129, 255 };

        printf("%s\n", nonstring);

        return(0);
}
```

Guess the Output

 Try to guess what the output is before moving to the next page.

If you're lucky, the output appears like this:

```
greetings, human0?u??
```

If you're unlucky, you see far more garbage spew all over the terminal window. In some rare cases you may see nothing, depending on the code page or font used for the terminal window.

Discussion

Character array nonstring[] is a collection of single characters. It's not a string. The final character in the array is 'n' and not the null character, '\0', which terminates a string.

When the printf() statement outputs the array as a string, it assumes that the string terminates with the null character. Because character array nonstring[] is unterminated, the printf() function continues to gobble characters, chewing along until it finds an accidental null character in the soupy garbage existing in memory. In the output above, that happenstance occurs after five random characters are output.

The point of this lesson is to always terminate strings. A character array is not a string. Only with the null character acting as a caboose does a collection of characters become a string. Remembering this admonition is vital when you create and manipulate your own strings. Many computer errors and security vulnerabilities exist due to improperly formed strings in C programming.

Nerdy Tidbits

The non-terminating non-string may output properly in some cases, though don't ever count on it. Most computer systems today allocate storage in 16-byte chunks. If a non-terminated string is less than this size, it may sit in a 16-byte chunk already filled with zeros, which terminates the string accidentally. This condition isn't anything you can take to the bank, but it may explain why some non-terminated strings work under these conditions.

In this chapter's code, the nonstring[] array contains exactly 16 characters, which I set on purpose so that it would fill a 16 byte memory chunk. The 16-byte boundary increases the chances that the next 16-byte chunk contains garbage or other information, which is output with the unterminated string.

Adding the data[] array also helps fill the next 16-byte chunk with preset "garbage."

The point to drive home is that a character array isn't a string unless the characters are terminated with the null character, \0.

Further Reading

General description and examples of character arrays and strings
> https://www.tutorialspoint.com/cprogramming/c_strings.htm

Null terminated string information, plus string functions
> http://www.cs.ecu.edu/karl/2530/spr17/Notes/C/String/nullterm.html

Review of string formation and rules regarding null terminated strings
> https://wiki.sei.cmu.edu/confluence/display/c/STR32-C.+Do+not+pass+a+non-null-terminat-
> ed+character+sequence+to+a+library+function+that+expects+a+string

Hello, stdin

```c
#include <stdio.h>

int main()
{
        char buffer[BUFSIZ]; /* BUFSIZ is a constant defined in stdio.h */

        setbuf(stdout, buffer);

        puts("Wait for it!");
        puts("Wait for it!");
        puts("Now!");
        getchar();
        puts("Whew!");

        return(0);
}
```

Guess the Output

Try to guess what the output is before moving to the next page.

No output is generated when the program starts. Press the ENTER key, and the following text appears:

```
Wait for it!
Wait for it!
Now!
Whew!
```

Discussion

I confess that you won't understand the output order unless you know what the setbuf() function does. Even if you don't, look at the presentation:

```
setbuf(stdout, buffer);
```

The first argument is the stdout constant, representing the standard output device. The second argument is the character array buffer. As the function is named "set buffer," a guess that it has something to do with output buffering would be correct.

In this instance, the setbuf() function alters output buffering so text isn't output until something floats in through standard input, for instance, the keypress. Once you press the Enter key, the buffer is flushed and you see the output.

Text Buffering

The setbuf() function uses three modes to control standard input/output buffering:

Unbuffered—The text output is sent to the output device immediately, with no waiting.

Block buffered—Text is saved in a buffer, waiting until the buffer is filled to send the text. The text is also sent once a newline character is encountered.

Line buffered—Text is saved in a buffer until the newline character is encountered or standard input is received.

The default mode is block buffered, though for terminals, text is line buffered. This type of buffering explains why you might expect to see three lines of text appear before the getchar() function paused output:

```
Wait for it!
Wait for it!
Now!
```

What the setbuf() function does in the sample code is to activate block buffering for standard output using the BUFSIZ value. (Constant BUFSIZ is defined in the stdio.h header file and used for buffered I/O.)

To set unbuffered text output, which you may desire for some interactive programs, use the setvbuf() function in this configuration:

```
setvbuf(stdout, buffer, _IONBUF,BUFSIZ);
```

This statement specifies the standard output device, stdout, and a character storage chunk named buffer of size BUFSIZ. The _IONBUF constant sets the buffering mode to unbuffered, meaning text writing to standard output appears immediately. Use this statement if you find yourself frustrated when program output isn't as peppy as you desire.

Stream I/O

Text mode programs written in C are not interactive. They rely upon stream input/output, where text flows in from standard input and out to standard output in a buffered manner, as described in this chapter. Yes, text can linger in the buffer until the buffer is full or the newline (Enter key) character is encountered.

If you truly want to code interactive programs, I recommend using the ncurses library for Linux/Unix/macOS. It provides immediate interaction with the keyboard as well as full-screen control over text output.

Further Reading

Forcing a text buffer to empty (flushing)
   https://c-for-dummies.com/blog/?p=3675

I/O buffering explained
   https://www.geeksforgeeks.org/i-o-buffering-and-its-various-techniques/

Understanding the fflush() function
   https://www.educative.io/answers/what-is-fflush-in-c

Loop Up and Down

```
#include <stdio.h>

int main()
{
        int u,d;

        for( u=0, d=0; u<11; u++, d-- )
                printf("%2d %2d\n", u, d);

        return(0);
}
```

Guess the Output

Try to guess what the output is before moving to the next page.

The code shows the output of both variables u and d as they ascend and descend from zero:

```
 0  0
 1 -1
 2 -2
 3 -3
 4 -4
 5 -5
 6 -6
 7 -7
 8 -8
 9 -9
10 -10
```

A single loop both initializes and increments/decrements each value, setting what could be multiple statements into the *for* loop statement itself.

Discussion

A for loop statement contains three parts, each separated by a semicolon:

- The initialization
- The terminating condition
- A statement to execute for each loop iteration

Each of these parts is optional. When missing, the compiler sticks a 1 or TRUE in its place, which creates an endless loop:

```
for(;;)
```

For the first and last items, you can set multiple expressions, separating each with a comma. The effect is to reduce the number of statements required before and in the loop. For example, this chapter's code could be expanded to read:

```
d = 0;
for( u=0; u<11; u++ )
{
        printf("%2d %2d\n", u, d);
        d--;
}
```

You need not set these statements outside the for loop, which tidies up the code. In fact, you could also do this:

```
for( u=0, d=0; u<11; u++, d--, printf("%2d %2d\n", u, d))
        ;
```

The printf() statement is also moved inside the for loop statement. Three expressions are set as the "while looping" part of the loop, each separated by a comma. The sole semicolon on the following line is required so the compiler does not flag the construction as a mistake. (Many beginners in the habit of ending each line with a semicolon may mistakenly create an empty loop.)

Warnings and Such

Not every statement in a for loop can be jammed into the statement, as shown in this chapter. Some expressions may cause the compiler to wince, in which case you must use the traditional for loop construction, holding statements in brackets.

Items set as the last item in a for loop statement may execute one more time after the loop has completed. This effect happens because these statements are executed before the exit condition is triggered.

I've not seen an example where multiple terminating conditions are specified, separated by commas. When two or more conditions can terminate a loop, a single expression composed of logical operators often handles the job.

Further Reading

In-depth discussion of loops in C, including break and continue
https://www.cprogramming.com/tutorial/c/lesson3.html

Overview of the for loop
https://en.cppreference.com/w/c/language/for

String Construction

```c
#include <stdio.h>

int main()
{
        char filename[] = "update.txt";
        char name[16];
        int x;

        /* initialize the name[] buffer with dots */
        for( x=0; x<16; x++ )
                name[x] = '.';

        /* extract first part of the filename */
        x = 0;
        while( filename[x] != '.' )
        {
                name[x] = filename[x];
                x++;
        }

        /* output result */
        printf("Extracted name '%s' from '%s'\n",
                        name,
                        filename
                );

        return(0);
}
```

Guess the Output

Try to guess what the output is before moving to the next page.

The code extracts the first part of a filename, before the extension. But it fails:

```
Extracted name 'update..........' from 'update.txt'
```

Discussion

This chapter's point is to drive home the importance of properly terminating strings you create. In the sample code, the first part of the filename is extracted and saved in a buffer—but without adding the \0 (null character) to mark the end of the string. Because the extracted string isn't terminated, the dots inside the buffer overflow and become part of the output. (It could look even worse than what's shown here because the initialized buffer lacks a terminating null character.)

As is often the case, the remainder of the buffer might be filled with zeros, which translate into the null character. If the code didn't bother initializing the name[] buffer, the output may look just fine:

```
Extracted name 'update' from 'update.txt'
```

In fact, this output—which looks correct but is improperly stored—has been the bane of C programs since its inception. These flaws are one reason why higher-level languages are preferred and why the Rust language is gaining ground on C for low-level programming. Unlike C, Rust doesn't let you cobble together an unterminated string.

The solution is rather simple. A single statement is added after the while loop:

```
name[x] = '\0';
```

The value of variable x is equal to the offset where the period is found in the filename[] string. Assigning this position to the null character effectively terminates the name[] string. With the string properly terminated, it can be used with various string functions and output just like any other string. The program is also more secure.

Other Observations and Notes

A good way to fix the code is to substitute the period with the null character at Line 11 when the name[] buffer is initialized:

```
name[x] = '\0';
```

This update ensures that a null character trails the string even if the string isn't terminated after the while loop. (But you should always terminate strings.)

Another item that bothers me is the size of the name[] buffer, which is set to 16. If I were coding this program for release into the wild, I would set name[] as a pointer and allocate its size based on the size of the original string in filename[]. This approach ensures that the buffer has enough space to store the first part of the filename without any overflow. Otherwise, when the array size is manually set, the programmer is just making a best guess as to its potential size. Such guessing in the C language is dangerous.

Further Reading

A historical perspective on the null-character terminated string
    https://queue.acm.org/detail.cfm?id=2010365

C language string tutorial
    https://www.geeksforgeeks.org/strings-in-c/

More Simple

```c
#include <stdio.h>
int main()
{
        int n, d, larger, smaller, diff;

        printf("Enter a fraction (nn/nn): ");
        scanf("%d/%d", &n, &d);

        printf("%d/%d = ", n, d);

        larger = n>d ? n : d;
        smaller = n<d ? n : d;
        diff = larger-smaller;

        while( diff!=larger)
        {
                larger = smaller>diff ? smaller : diff;
                smaller = smaller==larger ? diff : smaller;
                diff = larger-smaller;
        }

        if( diff>1 )
                printf("%d/%d\n", n/diff, d/diff);
        else
                printf("%d/%d\n", n, d);

        return(0);
}
```

Guess the Output

Try to guess what the output is before moving to the next page.

The code requires that you input two integers in the form of a fraction, such as: 21/63. Here is the output:

```
Enter a fraction (nn/nn): /*  user inputs 21/63 */
21/63 = 1/3
```

The fraction is reduced—simplified—if it can be. When the fraction can't be simplified, the original fraction is output.

Discussion

Computers are good at math, so you don't need to be! All you must know is the proper mathematical incantation, code it, and the computer does the work. When simplifying a fraction, you look for the greatest common divisor (GCD) between the two values. For 21 and 63, the value is 21 itself:

```
21 / 21 = 1
63 / 21 = 3
```

I've written code that seeks out the GCD in several ways. The first, rather brutish method is to discover the factors for each value. These are the integers that divide cleanly into each value.

For 21, the factors are 1, 3, 7, and 21.

For 63, the factors are 1, 3, 7, 9, 21, and 63.

Eyeballing it, you can see that 21 is the GCD for both values. Therefore, you divide both values by 21 to reduce the fraction 21/63 into 1/3.

To use the GCD method to simplify a faction, you first calculate and store the factors for each value, find the largest common one, and then divide by both values to obtain the result. But an easier way exists.

For this chapter's code, I used Euclid's algorithm to simplify the fractions. It works by taking the difference between the two values and repeatedly subtracting this difference until a new difference is calculated.

I'll use the fraction 42/56 as an example. The difference between the larger and smaller values is 14:

```
56 - 42 = 14
```

Subtract the difference (14) from the smaller value as many times as possible:

```
42 - 14 = 28
28 - 14 = 14
14 - 14 = 0
```

The value 14 is the GCD between 56 and 42. Divide each by 14 to behold the reduced fraction:

```
42 / 14 = 3
56 / 14 = 4
```

If the value left over is less than one, the fraction cannot be reduced. For example, 7/11 has this difference:

```
11 - 7 = 4
```

Then, the smaller value is reduced by four several times:

```
7 - 4 = 3
3 - 4 = -1
```

Because the final value is less than one, the algorithm states that the fraction cannot be reduced. This test is made in the code before the result is output.

I grant that the algorithm is difficult to explain. Yet, understanding the algorithm comes after being able to program it. The code contains many ternary decisions to determine which value is larger, and then the difference between the values is calculated repeatedly in a while loop until the values can no longer be reduced.

Further Reading

The Euclidean algorithm
> https://en.wikipedia.org/wiki/Euclidean_algorithm

Finding the greatest common divisor (GCD)
> https://www.cuemath.com/numbers/greatest-common-divisor-gcd/

Understanding factors
> https://www.splashlearn.com/math-vocabulary/multiplication/factor

Code a program to reveal factors for any positive integer
> https://c-for-dummies.com/blog/?p=3162

Whoa! Hold on There

```c
#include <stdio.h>
#include <stdlib.h>
#include <time.h>

int main()
{
        int array[5];
        int x;

        srand( (unsigned)time(NULL) );

        for( x=0; x<12; x++ )
        {
                array[x] = rand() % 100;
                printf(" %d", array[x]);
        }
        putchar('\n');

        return(0);
}
```

Guess the Output

Try to guess what the output is before moving to the next page.

The code fetches random numbers, packing them into an array and then outputting the results:

```
18 47 90 65 27 25 2 39 67 67 56 97
Segmentation fault (or some other fatal error)
```

Due to overflow, however, a segmentation fault or similar error is generated. Different compilers create programs that may display erroneous data, such as very large values. Some programs may run without any noticeable issue.

Discussion

Of all the major programming languages used today, C is the only one that doesn't automatically check array bounds. In the sample code, the array is allocated storage for five integers. The for loop assigns 12 integers to the array, which causes the program to explode. Other languages spot this problem right away and won't even compile the code, but not C.

What happens with the output varies depending on the machine. In rare cases, the program seems unaffected. This type of output is why some programmers don't notice the issue and how such programs are often exploited for security flaws.

In C, it's up to you (the programmer) to keep track of an array's size. You must constantly be aware of this limitation, lest your code plow through the end of the array and stomp over innocent, unprotected memory.

My suggestion to avoid this problem is to use constants to set array sizes. For example:

```
const int size = 5;
int array[size];
```

Some compilers may not like this construction, where a constant is used to dimension an array. In this case, you can use a defined constant instead. Set this line outside of any function:

```
#define SIZE 5
```

And then initialize the array like this:

```
int array[SIZE];
```

No matter how you do it, the for loop is then re-written with the size constant specified, not a literal value:

```
for( x=0; x<SIZE; x++ )
```

Not only does this construction avoid overflow, it makes the code more read-able and is self-documenting. Setting literals in your code (such as 5 for the array size) is referred to as using "magic numbers," which leads to confusion or, in this case, array overflow.

These same thoughts also apply to allocated storage. If your program needs a buffer on the fly, ensure that you use constants or a specific variable to track the size. Set safeguards in the code to ensure that this limit is never exceeded.

Another Quirk

Some compilers are clever enough to spot an out-of-bounds array reference when it's made directly. For example, if array[] is set to hold five elements, the compiler flags the following statement as out-of-bounds. Here's the warning message generated from the clang compiler:

```
08_holdon.c:11:1: warning: array index 10 is past the end of the array
(which contains 5 elements) [-Warray-bounds]
array[10] = 7;
^        ~~
08_holdon.c:7:2: note: array 'array' declared here
        int array[5];
        ^

1 warning generated.
```

The reference to array[10] (the 11th element) is out-of-bounds, and the compiler knows it. This type of warning helps avoid overflow, but it doesn't spot a for loop or other processing that may extend beyond the space allocated for the array.

Further Reading

The first Internet virus (worm) exploited a buffer flow
 https://en.wikipedia.org/wiki/Morris_worm

Good discussion on bounds checking in C
 https://balvant4u.wordpress.com/2015/10/08/array-bounds-checking-in-c/

Say It Again—Or Not

```c
#include <stdio.h>

int main()
{
        int a = 11;

        do
        {
                printf("a = %d\n", a);
                a--;
        }
        while(a<10);

        return(0);
}
```

Guess the Output

Try to guess what the output is before moving to the next page.

The loop repeats once despite the value of variable a being greater than the loop's terminating condition:

```
a = 11
```

Discussion

The point of this exercise is to recognize that do-while loops always run at least once, no matter what the terminating condition, but more is going on in the code. In the sample code, the initial value of variable a is 11. The loop repeats while its value is less than 10. Had this construction been a straight while loop, none of the statements would have been executed. But for a do-while loop, the statements always execute at least once.

The output may have caught you by surprise. When I wrote the code, I expected the output to show variable a equal to 10:

```
a = 10
```

After all, the statement a--; in the code decrements the value of a from its initial assignment of 11 down to 10, right? It does, of course. But the value is output in a printf() statement before it's decremented. Therefore, the final value of variable a is 10, but the output value is 11. You can take advantage of this effect for any loop in your code.

It's consistent that a looping variable's value after the loop has a direct relationship with the loop's terminating condition. Consider this for loop:

```
for( a=0; a<10; a++ )
```

The for loop repeats ten times, incrementing variable a from zero to nine until it stops. At that point, the value of variable a is equal to 10. Many programmers may hold that the variable's value is 9, which makes sense within the loop. But after the loop is done, variable a is equal to 10.

I often take advantage of a looping variable's value after the loop, especially when manipulating a string. After the loop's conclusion, the looping variable references the character position after the last character in the string. This position makes it easy to terminate the string, for example:

```
*a = '\0';
```

You must trust that this observation is consistent and correct: after a loop, the looping variable's value is based upon the loop's terminating condition—even for a do-while loop.

Further Reading

Introduction to looping in C programs
https://www.guru99.com/c-loop-statement.html

Good discussion on do-while loops
https://www.scaler.com/topics/c/do-while-loop-in-c/

Deciphering scanf()

```c
#include <stdio.h>

int main()
{
        char buffer[32];

        printf("Type something: ");
        scanf("%[ABC]", buffer);
        printf("You typed: %s\n", buffer);

        return(0);
}
```

Guess the Output

Try to guess what the output is before moving to the next page.

The program prompts for input, but only uppercase letters ABC are allowed:

```
Type something: ALPHA
You typed: A
```

Any character input other than ABC (in any order) terminates input.

Discussion

I'm not a fan of the scanf() function. It's a formatted input function, so it's not well suited for reading text input, though it's often used this way in introductory programming books and courses. (I use fgets() instead.)

No, the f in scanf() stands for *formatted*. The input is formatted in a manner similar to the way the printf() function formats output. With streaming input, however, the formatting works differently.

Instead of thinking of formatted input, think of scanf() as an input *filtering* function. Only those characters or data types listed in the formatting string are allowed as input. Anything outside the specified format terminates input.

For example, the %s placeholder filters string input but not whitespace. When a whitespace character is encountered, the scanf() function stops reading input.

The %[...] and %[^...] placeholders are unique to the scanf() function. These are character input filters that allow or restrict input to only those characters specified. Many programmers are unaware of these filters, and along with my general disdain for the scanf() function, these filters are rarely used.

The %[...] placeholder filters input to only those characters set within the brackets. The characters are case-sensitive. Any character in the input string that is not specified terminates the input. For the %[ABC] placeholder, you can type as many As, Bs, and Cs as you like in any order. When a character other than A, B, or C is encountered, input is terminated.

A useful example of this placeholder might be this statement:

```
scanf("%[$1234567890.,]", buffer);
```

Valid input includes the characters specified, which might be ideal for reading a monetary amount.

The %[^...] placeholder allows for all characters input except those specified. Any character found in the %[^...] placeholder terminates input. In fact, this placeholder can be used to direct scanf() to input a full string, including whitespace characters:

```
scanf("%[^\n]", buffer);
```

The statement above reads all characters into the char array buffer[] up to the newline. The newline is not included in the string, but any whitespace characters are, which makes this the rare way of convincing the scanf() function to read a string.

Caveat Programmator

The scanf() function is not considered secure. The function exhibits undefined behavior when input doesn't match the data type specified. Further, without any input bounds checking, it's possible to overflow a string buffer. No, I recommend that you avoid scanf() and craft your own functions that defend and validate input.

Further Reading

Overview of the scanf() function and its various siblings
https://en.cppreference.com/w/c/io/fscanf

The scanf() function and safe coding practices
https://c-for-dummies.com/blog/?p=2812

What is Nothing?

```
#include <stdio.h>

int main()
{
        float n, p;

        n = -0.0;
        p = +0.0;

        if( n==p )
                printf("negative zero is equal to positive zero\n");
        else
                printf("negative zero is not equal to positive zero\n");

        return(0);
}
```

Guess the Output

 Try to guess what the output is before moving to the next page.

The code compares negative and positive zero as created by the compiler and stored in memory:

```
negative zero is equal to positive zero
```

Discussion

In C programming, negative zero and positive zero are identical.

I'm not a mathematician, but I enjoy reading about math. For example, I've read that zero is considered an even number. Zero is not the same as infinity. Also, zero isn't considered positive or negative—unless it's used in a programming language such as Java.

In C, however, zero is considered zero, even when you prefix it with a sign operator, as is done in this chapter's sample code. Unlike other real numbers, C doesn't encode a sign bit when storing floating point value zero—even though you can use a sign bit when assigning a zero to a variable.

Zero and Null

Zero and NULL are not the same thing in C programming, even though they both smell and taste alike. Plus, they play a role in the value of zero.

The NULL constant is defined in the stdio.h header file. It's a pointer, referencing an unknown or unassigned memory location. Even though its value may technically be zero, NULL is not memory address zero. Do not think of it as zero!

Toss into the mix the null character, \0. Yes, this escape character does represent ASCII character code zero. It's not the same null as the pointer constant NULL, which is one reason why I write them in different cases.

Further Reading

Numberphile's explanation of positive and negative zero
https://www.youtube.com/watch?v=8t1TC-5OLdM

The concept of "signed zero" in programming
https://dbpedia.org/page/Signed_zero

A discussion on the difference between zero and NULL
https://www.differencebetween.info/difference-between-zero-and-null

On the Case

```
#include <stdio.h>

int main()
{
        char a;

        for( a='A'; a<='Z'; a++ )
                putchar( a | 0x20 );
        putchar('\n');

        for( a='a'; a<='z'; a++ )
                putchar( a & 0xdf );
        putchar('\n');

        return(0);
}
```

Guess the Output

Try to guess what the output is before moving to the next page.

Two lines are output:

```
abcdefghijklmnopqrstuvwxyz
ABCDEFGHIJKLMNOPQRSTUVWXYZ
```

The uppercase letters are converted into lowercase. Lowercase letters are converted to uppercase.

Discussion

Most C programmers rush to the ctype functions when letters need case conversions. The toupper() and tolower() functions handle the job nicely. Yet, because of the way the ASCII is designed, you can use bitwise logical operators to manipulate case, as shown in this chapter.

In the ASCII table, the difference between an uppercase letter and its lowercase counterpart is 32 or 0x20 hexadecimal:

A is 0x41 or 0100 0001

a is 0x61 or 0110 0001

Flipping that sixth bit (from the right) transforms the character from uppercase to lowercase and back again. In C programming, if you want to flip a bit, you use bitwise logical operators, such as & (AND) and | (OR).

The bitwise OR operator sets a bit. In the code, | 0x20 sets the sixth bit, which punches up the value of characters A through Z to lowercase a through z.

The bitwise AND operator filters out a bit. In the code, & 0xdf resets the sixth bit to zero, which transforms lowercase a through z into uppercase A through Z.

Unlike the ctype toupper() and tolower() functions, however, this trick affects all ASCII characters, not just letters. While it's not a complete replacement, this bit manipulation trick can be used to quickly and efficiently change case for letters of the alphabet.

Further Reading

ASCII everything
https://www.asciitable.com/

History of coded character sets (PDF document)
https://textfiles.meulie.net/bitsaved/Books/Mackenzie_CodedCharSets.pdf

C programming tutorial on bitwise operators
https://www.programiz.com/c-programming/bitwise-operators

Bits and Pieces

```c
#include <stdio.h>
int main()
{
        int a, b;

        printf("Enter a positive integer: ");
        scanf("%d", &a);

        b = ~a + 1;

        printf("Result: %d\n", b);

        return(0);
}
```

Guess the Output

Try to guess what the output is before moving to the next page.

The user types a positive value, and then the program outputs the negative for that value:

```
Enter a positive integer: 12345
Result: -12345
```

Changing the sign for an integer value is done by using binary manipulation, resetting the sign bit and adjusting the final value by one to equal the negative of the value input.

Discussion

To understand this chapter's code, you must know two things: first, how the computer stores signed integers, and second, how the two's complement operator works at the binary level.

A signed integer uses the far-left bit, the sign bit, to indicate a positive or negative value. When the sign bit is zero (unset), the value is positive. When the sign bit is one (set), the value is negative. For example:

5 in binary is 0000 0101

-5 in binary is 1111 1011

You might think that -5 would be coded as 1000 0101, as the sign bit is set for a negative value and the rest of the bits represent five. But that's not how it works! If you add one to the value 1000 0101, you get 1000 0110, which by the same rules translates to -6. Both examples are wrong.

Binary math is weirdly interesting, but it's not something you need to concern yourself with unless you decide to dive into bits at a low level.

The ~ operator manipulates an integer at the binary level by flipping all its bits: all the zeros become ones and all the ones become zeros. This operation helps convert a positive value to a negative value, but it's only the first step.

If you apply the ~ operator to the value five, you get:

5 in binary is 0000 0101

~5 in binary is 1111 1010

The binary value 1111 1010 is -6, which is one less than -5. So, to complete the operation, you must add one to the result. The algorithm works like this:

1. Take the two's complement of the original value (use the ~ operator)
2. Add one to the result (++)

This algorithm also works when converting negative integers into their positive equivalents, which is one of the nifty things about the way negative values are encoded in binary.

In the sample code, this operation takes place in this expression:

```
b = ~a + 1;
```

Of course, in C, you can use the sign operator to obtain the negative value of any integer:

```
b = -a;
```

But the point of this exercise is to show how C manipulates data at the binary level and hopefully expand your knowledge of bits and data encoding. If you enjoy programming in C, someday this knowledge tidbit will come in handy.

A final point to note is that some large values may translate to negative for certain signed integer data types. For example, a signed character value of 255 may translate into -1. Values may overflow as well, so a signed character variable assigned the value 256 may only hold 1 as its value.

Further Reading

Binary tutorial, negative numbers, and the one's and two's complement math thingies
https://ryanstutorials.net/binary-tutorial/binary-negative-numbers.php

Two's complement description, including two's complement arithmetic
https://www.cs.cornell.edu/~tomf/notes/cps104/twoscomp.html

Bitwise math
https://pro.arcgis.com/en/pro-app/latest/tool-reference/spatial-analyst/how-bitwise-math-tools-work.htm

Teeny Tiny Math

```
#include <stdio.h>

int main()
{
        int a;

        printf("Enter an integer: ");
        scanf("%d", &a);

        printf("%d\n", a<<1);
        printf("%d\n", a>>1);

        return(0);
}
```

Guess the Output

Try to guess what the output is before moving to the next page.

The bit shift operators manipulate the value input, first doubling it and then halving it.

```
Enter an integer: 20
40
10
```

When 20 is input, the first value output is double, 40. The second value output is halved, 10. Odd values divided by two are rounded to the next integer.

Discussion

C is often considered a mid-level language—and it has the bitwise operators to prove it. Two of my favorites are the shift operators, << and >>. These tools manipulate data at the bit level, marching bits to the left or right (respectively), which has a mathematical effect on the integer value.

The shift-left (<<) operator increases an integer's value by powers of two, based on the shift value. For example, <<1 shifts the bits left one notch, multiplying the value by two:

0110 0001 (97)

Becomes:

1100 0010 (194)

Using <<2 shifts the bits over two spots, multiplying the value by four or 2^2:

0000 1111 (15)

Becomes:

0011 1100 (60)

The shift-right (>>) operator decreases an integer's value, also by powers of two. Of course, the value is rounded when it doesn't divide evenly. With >>1, the value is cut in half:

0010 0000 (32)

Becomes:

0001 0000 (16)

Here's an odd number, shifted thrice (3^2):

0011 0010 (50)

After >>3, the value is:

0000 1100 (12)

Bits that are shifted "off the end" are discarded; they don't wrap around. Zero bits are added right or left, depending on the shift direction. This effect doesn't quite make the shifting operation a clean division, which is what to expect when dealing with integers.

It's possible to stack these operations to perform basic multiplication and division beyond powers of two. For example, to multiply an integer by ten, you shift it left three times (multiplying it by eight), then add the result of shifting it left once (multiplying it by two). For example:

1^2 is two

8 + 2 = 10

```
b = (a<<3) + (a<<1);
```

The above statement assigns the value of variable b to ten times the value of variable a: a<<3 is a3^2 *or a*8, plus* a1^2 or a*2. Because 8+2=10, the result is multiplying variable a by ten, a*10.

Some Caveats

While this binary math is interesting, and at the processor level it's faster than using the multiplication and division operators, the results can be off. Shifting right results in rounding errors, and shifting left may overflow, resulting in an inaccurate result.

If you input a negative value, the sample code may accurately reflect the doubled and halved result—or it may not. Bit-shifting negative numbers results in undefined behavior.

Finally, be aware that in the C++ language, the insertion and extraction operators look exactly like the bit-shifting operators in C. The difference in interpretation depends upon the order of evaluation.

Further Reading

Binary math, including examples
https://www.binarymath.info/

Bit shifting operators
https://www.geeksforgeeks.org/left-shift-right-shift-operators-c-cpp/

More bitwise operators in C and their descriptions
https://www.geeksforgeeks.org/bitwise-operators-in-c-cpp/

It Just Can't Be Done

```
#include <stdio.h>

int main()
{
        char a;

        for( a=0; a<200; a++ )
                printf("%3d ", a);
        putchar('\n');

        return(0);
}
```

Guess the Output

Try to guess what the output is before moving to the next page.

Ignoring any error the compiler coughs up, the program outputs an endless loop, cycling from zero to 127, then from -128 to zero again. Press Ctrl+C to halt the nonsense.

Discussion

The moral of this chapter's story is to always use unsigned variables in a loop that counts things. The code runs properly when you add the keyword unsigned before the variable declaration:

```
unsigned char a;
```

After performing this modification, the loop ticks from zero to 199, reflected in the output.

Another solution is to use a larger data type, such as short or int instead of char. Remember, in C you can output a character as an integer if you use the %d conversion character in a printf() statement. Providing that the character code is displayable, it outputs just fine.

An issue tangential to this chapter's endless loop code is when you want to loop the entire char data type range in a loop. For example, assuming that a is an unsigned char data type:

```
for( a=0; a<256; a++ )
```

The range for an unsigned char data type is from zero through 255. A smart compiler (such as clang) recognizes that 256 is out of range for an unsigned char and should flag this statement with an "always true" warning. Even if you modify the statement, however, an endless loop is still generated:

```
for( a=0; a<=255; a++ )
```

While the condition a<=255 does keep the test within the range of an unsigned char variable, a for loop's construction causes variable a to increment after it reaches the value 255. The next value "after" 255 in an unsigned char range is zero, so the loop continues to repeat endlessly.

If you must use an unsigned char variable to loop from zero to 255, the solution is to provide a test within the loop to signal the exit condition:

```
if( a==255 ) break;
```

This approach works for both for and while loops, assuming that variable a is an unsigned char.

Further Reading

C language data types, sizes, ranges
> https://www.studytonight.com/c/datatype-in-c.php

Loop reference, for loop
> https://en.cppreference.com/w/c/language/for

The char data type
> https://mathcenter.oxford.emory.edu/site/cs170/charType/

Misallocation

```c
#include <stdio.h>
#include <stdlib.h>
#include <string.h>

int main()
{
        struct raw { int value; char string[32]; };
        FILE *outfile;
        struct raw *data;

        /* allocate and fill the structure */
        data = malloc( sizeof(struct raw) );
        data->value = 60;
        strcpy( data->string, "This is a string\n" );

        /* open a file and save the data */
        outfile = fopen("data.dat","w");
        if( outfile==NULL )
                exit(1);
        fwrite(&data, sizeof(data), 1, outfile);
        fclose(outfile);
        puts("File written");

        /* clean up */
        free(data);
        return(0);
}
```

Guess the Output

Try to guess what the output is before moving to the next page.

I hope you guessed this line as the output:

```
File written
```

It's true, the file was written. The question is, what was written? The *hexdump* program can confirm what was written. Here is that program's output:

```
$ hexdump data.dat
0000000 d2a0 d9a9 5570 0000
0000008
```

Does it look like the text This is a string is nestled somewhere in those bytes? Hmmm.

Discussion

Structures are fun. Pointers to structures can spoil the fun because many C programmers don't understand (or take the effort to understand) pointers. This confusion leads to a common problem when allocating storage or, as is the case in this chapter's code, setting the size of a data chunk to be written to a file.

Here is the offending statement in the code:

```
fwrite(&data, sizeof(data), 1, outfile);
```

This fwrite() call is successful. The argument &data sets the address for the buffer to be written; sizeof(data) sets the size; 1 is the number of chunks to write, and outfile is the open file handle. The problem lies in the second argument, the size of the chunk to write.

The raw structure is defined at Line 7. Pointer variable data is declared at Line 9. It's of the raw structure type—but it's a pointer, not a structure. If it weren't a pointer, the code would properly write the data to the file—all of the data. But because variable data is a pointer, the sizeof operator returns the pointer's size in memory, an address.

To fix the code, you must use the sizeof operator on the raw structure, not the data pointer variable:

```
fwrite(&data, sizeof(raw), 1, outfile);
```

On my computer, the raw structure occupies 36 bytes of storage: four for the integer variable and 32 for the string. The data pointer occupies eight bytes of storage, the size of an address on my machine.

Even when I'm not using pointers, I always refer to the structure definition and not the variable when allocating or referring to storage size. Use this choice anytime the sizeof operator is required.

Further Reading

How a structure's size plays into memory alignment
https://c-for-dummies.com/blog/?p=2477

Details on the sizeof operator
https://en.cppreference.com/w/c/language/sizeof

Eenie, Meenie, Miney, Mod

```c
#include <stdio.h>

int main()
{
        int m = 1;

        while( m<10 )
        {
                if( 2%m )
                        printf("%d - Odd\n", m);
                else
                        printf("%d - Even\n", m);
                m++;
        }

        return(0);
}
```

Guess the Output

Try to guess what the output is before moving to the next page.

The program displays the following output:

```
1 - Even
2 - Even
3 - Odd
4 - Odd
5 - Odd
6 - Odd
7 - Odd
8 - Odd
9 - Odd
```

Discussion

The modulo operator (%) returns the remainder of the first number divided by the second: 5 % 3 results in two, the remainder of 5 ÷ 3. While such expressions are interesting, the true power of the modulo, or "mod," operator is that it counts intervals.

In the case of "mod two," your program can alternate odd and even values, for example, to highlight every other row. This expression works as long as you remember the modulo operator mantra: *The larger value goes first.*

The problem with the sample code is that the smaller value is first. The result is that the remainder is calculated based on an increasing value (variable m), which results in the unusual output.

If you swap the values in the expression at Line 9 to read m%2, you see this output:

```
1 - Odd
2 - Even
3 - Odd
4 - Even
5 - Odd
6 - Even
7 - Odd
8 - Even
9 - Odd
```

The result of m%2 is equal to one for odd number values. This output is correct, whereas if you mess up the expression's order, you see unpredictable output, as shown on the preceding page.

Nerdy Tidbits

In the sample code, variable m is initialized to one. If m starts at zero, the program crashes as 2%m attempts to divide two by zero. This result occurred when I first coded the program. The "segmentation fault" error threw me until I walked through the code and realized it attempted to divide by zero.

If you code the expression properly, m%2, and you start with m at zero, you see that zero is an even number. This classification is true in mathematics, as zero follows all the rules for even numbers.

Further Reading

Making the modulo operator fun
 https://www.mathsisfun.com/numbers/modulo.html

Dividing by zero and why computers can't
 https://www.centralgalaxy.com/division-by-zero/

Is zero an odd or even number?
 https://www.britannica.com/story/is-zero-an-even-or-an-odd-number

Superhero's Secret Identity

```c
#include <stdio.h>

#define SIZE 5

int main()
{
        int values[SIZE] = {2, 3, 5, 8, 13};
        int *v, x;

        /* initialize the pointer */
        v = values;

        for( x=0; x<SIZE; x++ )
        {
                printf("%2d = %2d\n",
                                values[x],
                                *(v+x)
                        );
        }

        return(0);
}
```

Guess the Output

Try to guess what the output is before moving to the next page.

The code uses both array and pointer notation to output the first five Fibonacci numbers:

```
 2 =  2
 3 =  3
 5 =  5
 8 =  8
13 = 13
```

Discussion

Arrays and pointers are similar but not exactly interchangeable. This relationship explains why many beginning C programmers use arrays as a replacement for pointers. Doing so can get you into trouble. But the point of this chapter is to show the easy conversion method between array and pointer notation.

Pointers are variables that hold a memory location, an address. A pointer can be considered a base, like an array's name. In the sample code, both values[] and v reference the same chunk of memory. The similarity between array notation and pointer notation to reference the integer values appears in the printf() statement: values[x] translates to *(v+x).

In both instances, variable x refers to an offset. It's an element number in array notation and an address offset in pointer notation: v+x is the base of the memory chunk (v) plus a given number of integer increments (x). This address is wrapped in parentheses and dereferenced by the * operator.

Tips and Traps

The relationship between array notation and pointers works only in one direction. You cannot assign a memory chunk address held in a pointer variable to an array. For example, assuming values[] is an array and v is a pointer:

```
values = v;
```

If you attempt such an assignment, the compiler gets all huffy and tosses an error in your direction.

However, it's possible to use array notation in a function where a pointer is passed as an argument.

```
void output(int *v)
{
        printf("%d\n", v[0]);
}
```

If the output() function accepts an integer pointer v, you can use v[] notation in the function to reference the memory chunk's data. Above, pointer v references a spot in memory containing integer values. Within the function, v[0] represents the first integer stored at memory location v. You could also use *(v+0) with the same result.

Further Reading

The relationship between pointers and arrays
> https://www.w3schools.com/c/c_pointers_arrays.php

Comparing pointers and arrays
> https://www.codingninjas.com/codestudio/library/difference-between-arrays-and-pointers

Good Q&A on pointers and arrays
> https://c-faq.com/aryptr/

Cursing Recursion

```c
#include <stdio.h>

long result(long v)
{
        if( v>1 )
                return(v*result(v-1));
        return(v);
}

int main()
{
        long a,r;

        printf("Enter a positive integer: ");
        scanf("%ld", &a);

        r = result(a);
        printf("The result is %ld\n", r);

        return(0);
}
```

Guess the Output

Try to guess what the output is before moving to the next page.

The code outputs the factorial for the value input. For example, five:

```
Enter a positive integer: 5
The result is 120
```

Discussion

Recursion is a programming concept that works like a loop. But instead of a chunk of code repeating, a function calls itself over and over—like a drunken ex who just can't let go, but with all the logic you expect from computer programming.

As with a loop, a terminating condition exists for a recursive function. When it's encountered, the recursion unwinds: the function returns to itself again and again until it eventually returns to the caller.

Indeed, recursion truly is insane, but it offers many practical solutions for adept coders who understand the insanity and can manipulate it in a beneficial manner.

The sample code uses recursion to calculate the factorial of a positive integer. This mathematical concept is the product of consecutive integers represented by the exclamation point, as in 5!. The 5! factorial works out to: 5 × 4 × 3 × 2 × 1. The result is 120.

In the sample code, the result() function accepts a long int argument and returns the factorial through recursion. The insanity happens in the if decision:

```
if( v>1 )
        return(v*result(v-1));
```

The trigger to release recursion is when the value of v is equal to one. Otherwise, when v is greater than one, the function multiplies variable v by the result of the return value of result(), but with v-1 as the argument.

As the function returns, the reduced value of v is multiplied by one less than v, over and over. The final return sends the result back to the caller.

The Fears and Delights of Recursion

When I first learned to code, I dreaded recursion. Not because I didn't understand it, but because I know how function calls work in a programming language. When a function keeps calling itself, it adds data to the stack. Eventually, the stack can overflow, which is a Bad Thing.

For example, if a recursive function lacks an ending condition, the stack will overflow. If you change the sample code for this chapter to read if(1), the program compiles and runs but eventually terminates with a segmentation fault.

The key to writing a good recursive function is to always ensure that it terminates.

It's not necessary to make the recursive call within a return statement, but doing so often resolves other issues that make the recursive function more complex.

It also helps to look at each recursive function call as a new version (or you can use the term "instance") of the function. This revelation helps us understand how the recursive function unwinds. For example, when the value v is equal to four, it remains equal to four when the recursive call returns to that one instance of the function.

Recursive functions work best in situations that call for repetitive tasks, like opening boxes inside boxes or navigating through a maze. In fact, a good example of a recursive function you can write on your own is one that plows the depths of subdirectories: the function works through a directory until it finds a subdirectory, then it calls itself.

Finally, be aware that though the stack may not implode, the recursive function may result in overflow if the output is too big for the variable it is assigned to. For example, running this chapter's program with an input value of 27 results in an overflow value of -5483646897237262336. If you want to calculate larger values, choose a larger data type.

Further Reading

Introduction to recursion
> https://c-for-dummies.com/blog/?p=1060

Real-world examples of recursion
> https://www.byte-by-byte.com/understanding-recursion/

A quick guide to recursion
> https://www.educative.io/blog/recursion

Time to Pull Out Your Hair

```c
#include <stdio.h>

void modify(char *c)
{
        *(c+1) = 'o';
}

int main()
{
        char *string = "cat";

        printf("Before: %s\n", string);
        modify(string);
        printf("After: %s\n", string);

        return(0);
}
```

Guess the Output

Try to guess what the output is before moving to the next page.

The output might be a surprise:

```
Before: cat
Segmentation fault
```

Discussion

Yes, it's a pointer problem. It's just not the pointer problem you may think it is. The issue lies in the construction of the string "cat." While you can declare a string as a pointer, you shouldn't do much with it. In fact, when I use such strings in my code, I declare them constant:

```
const char *string = "cat";
```

The const classifier forces the compiler to ensure that you don't further mess with the string beyond outputting it, copying it, or other forms of manipulation that don't alter it.

If your desire is to mess with the string, you can declare it as a pointer and then allocate the pointer. But a more practical solution is to declare the string as an array:

```
char string[] = "cat";
```

Array notation doesn't present a problem; this string can be manipulated anywhere within the code.

What's Going On?

The pointer string construction apparently exists in memory outside of the heap where other variables are stored. This arrangement means that you can manipulate the string—but not change it.

To show how the pointer string is set in an unusual memory location, use the %p placeholder to output the string's address in a printf() statement. For example:

```
char *cat = "cat";
char dog[] = "dog";

printf("Address of cat: %p\n", cat);
printf("Address of dog: %p\n", dog);
```

When run, the output shows radically different locations for each variable. On my system, I see:

```
Address of cat: 0x55ce84508004
Address of dog: 0x7ffff0477d6c
```

Variable dog is stored in the heap along with other program variables. Lord only knows where cat is stored. My guess is that it's in the code segment, which is marked as "read-only" and protected from modification. Regardless, and even if I'm incorrect in my assumptions, such a string construction cannot be altered. Use it if you must, but remember its limitations.

Further Reading

Types of memory in C programming
https://craftofcoding.wordpress.com/2015/12/07/memory-in-c-the-stack-the-heap-and-static/

Dealing with pointer-created string literals
https://wiki.sei.cmu.edu/confluence/display/c/STR05-C.+Use+pointers+to+const+when+referring+to+string+literals

You See It Everywhere

```c
#include <stdio.h>

int main()
{
    int f, n;
    int count;

    f = n = 1;
    count=0;
    while( count < 20 )
    {
        printf("%d ", f);
        f+=n;
        printf("%d ", n);
        n+=f;
        count+=2;
    }
        putchar('\n');

    return(0);
}
```

Guess the Output

Try to guess what the output is before moving to the next page.

The code outputs the first 20 values of the Fibonacci sequence:

1 1 2 3 5 8 13 21 34 55 89 144 233 377 610 987 1597 2584 4181 6765

Discussion

Named for Italian mathematician Leonardo Bonacci, also known as Fibonacci, the Fibonacci sequence is a series of values, each the sum of the preceding two values. The numbers in this sequence are referred to as *Fibonacci numbers*.

The Fibonacci series appears often in nature, art, and design. It's expressed mathematically in a variety of ways, but the best way to view and understand the series is visually, as illustrated below.

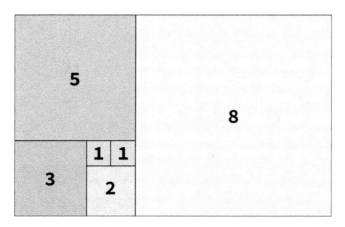

In the sample code, two variables are used to calculate the Fibonacci sequence, f and n. These variables are initialized to one and then put to work in a loop. Variable count sets the quantity of Fibonacci numbers to output.

I wanted to use only two variables to calculate the Fibonacci sequence, so the loop features two printf() statements to output the values and two expressions to calculate the next numbers in the series: f+=n and n+=f. As with the series itself, these variables build upon each other's values, working the series.

Further Reading

Understanding the Fibonacci sequence
> https://www.imaginationstationtoledo.org/about/blog/the-fibonacci-sequence

How breeding rabbits inspired Fibonacci
　　https://www.techtarget.com/whatis/definition/Fibonacci-sequence

Other ways to code the Fibonacci sequence
　　https://www.programiz.com/c-programming/examples/fibonacci-series

Using Binet's formula to calculate the Fibonacci sequence
　　https://www.codedrome.com/fibonacci-binets-formula-in-c/

3.14159 Etc.

```
#include <stdio.h>

float p(float a, float b)
{
        return((b<100.0)?a+(b*b/p(a+2.0, b+1.0)):b*b);
}

int main()
{
        printf("%.7f\n", 4.0/p(1.0, 1.0));
        return(0);
}
```

Guess the Output

Try to guess what the output is before moving to the next page.

Obviously, from the chapter title, you can guess that the output might have something to do with the value π—and it does:

3.1415925

How the code generates this output, especially without using any trigonometric functions, is the story to tell.

Discussion

Calculating π (pi), the ratio of a circle's diameter to its circumference, is an age-old computer programming task. I remember that episode of *Star Trek* where Mr. Spock directed the computer to "calculate to the last digit the value of pi." Of course, the computer got busy with the project to the point of pushing out an evil entity. O, computers can do amazing things!

The question isn't whether a computer can calculate the value of π but how? To assist the programmer, various mathematical theorems are available. Each of these is clever and cryptic, though the point is translating them from arithmetic hieroglyphics into C code.

For this chapter's program, I use the technique of a generalized continuing fraction, which is illustrated below.

$$\pi = \cfrac{4}{1 + \cfrac{1^2}{3 + \cfrac{2^2}{5 + \cfrac{3^2}{7 + \cfrac{4^2}{9 + \ddots}}}}}$$

While such a beast looks intimidating, it's quite elegant when you try to fish out the patterns: The numerator starts at four, but then the values are one squared, two squared, incrementing by one each time. The denominator starts at one and continues with odd numbers.

The structure of the continuing fraction begs for implementation as a recursive function: 4/1 plus 2^1>/3 plus and so on. In the code, this continuing fraction is represented by this expression:

```
a+(b*b/p(a+2.0, b+1.0))
```

Variable a is the denominator and b is the numerator. The fraction continues by calling function p() recursively with a+2.0 and b+1.0. (The decimal portion is added to direct the compiler to create floating-point literals.)

A ternary operator makes decisions in the recursive function. The test is b<100.0, which means recursion continues while the value of variable b is less than 100. When this condition is true, the function is called recursively, as described earlier. Otherwise, the value b*b is calculated, which is 2^b. This operation ends the continued fraction.

Eventually, recursive function p() unwinds, and the result is returned, with the value of π accurate to six digits.

Other methods of calculating π also lend themselves to interesting programming solutions. I've also used the Wallis product, which is linked to at the end of this chapter.

Fun π Programming

If you're desperate for the value of π in your code, you don't need to do any calculations. The math.h header file contains the definition M_PI, which is equal to this value:

```
3.14159265358979323846264338327950288
```

Keep in mind that NASA's Jet Propulsion Laboratory uses a value of π accurate to 15 digits to make its space flight calculations. The rest of the values just stimulate the math nerds.

Further Reading

All about yummy π
https://www.britannica.com/science/pi-mathematics

Using the Wallis product to calculate π
https://c-for-dummies.com/blog/?p=4042

Radians and degrees, or using π to calculate angles
https://medium.com/star-gazers/what-are-radians-a-simple-explanation-of-radian-vs-degree-565062445f69

Forget the sqrt() Function

```c
#include <stdio.h>
double babylonian(double r)
{
        double low, high;
        int x;
        const int precision = 7;

        low = 1.0;
        high = r;
        for( x=0; x<precision; x++ )
        {
                high = (high+low)/2.0;
                low = r/high;
        }
        return(low);
}

int main()
{
        double pv, sr;

        printf("Enter a positive value: ");
        scanf("%lf", &pv);
        if( pv <= 0 )
                return(1);
        sr = babylonian(pv);
        printf("The result is %f\n", sr);

        return(0);
}
```

Guess the Output

Try to guess what the output is before moving to the next page.

The code uses the Babylonian method to calculate a square root:

```
Enter a positive value: 7
The result is 2.645751
```

The square root of seven is 2.645751 (plus change).

Discussion

Most people learn how to perform long division but quickly forget how to calculate a square root. Even if you remember the way you were taught, many other techniques exist to calculate a square root.

As a reminder, a square root of a number is a value which, when multiplied by itself, yields the original number: the square root of 16 is four because $4 \times 4 = 16$. From the example, $2.645751 \times 2.645751 = 7$ (or close enough).

The Babylonian method is perhaps one of the most ingenious ways to reveal a number's square root. The steps work like this:

1: Start with the positive integer to find its square root.

From the input in this chapter, suppose it's 7.

2: Obtain the average of two values, one being greater than the positive integer and the second being less than what the integer's square root might be.

Without getting complex, choose one (1) as the low value and then the number itself (7) as the high value. The average of these two values is:

```
(7 + 1) / 2 = 4
```

Four becomes the new "high" value.

3: Divide the original value (7) by the result of step 2:

```
7 / 4 = 1.75
```

The result, 1.75, becomes the new "low" value.

4: Repeat steps 2 and 3 using the new high and low values:

```
(4 + 1.75) / 2 = 5.75
7 / 5.75 = 1.217
```

Repeat steps 2 and 3 again with the new high and low values:

```
(5.75 + 1.217) / 2 = 3.483
7 / 3.483 = 2.009
```

And so on. In the code, these calculations appear using variables high and low as follows, with variable r representing the original value:

```
high = (high+low)/2.0;
low = r/high;
```

Variable precision tracks how many times to repeat this operation, which is set to seven as a constant:

```
const int precision = 7;
```

The more you run the operation (repeating steps 2 and 3), the more precise the results, though after a while, the digits lose significance and the result is "close enough."

The final low value returned from the babylonian() function is the square root.

Further Reading

Squares and square roots
> https://www.expii.com/t/square-root-definition-examples-4586

The Babylonian method for finding square roots
> https://blogs.sas.com/content/iml/2016/05/16/babylonian-square-roots.html

Another way to find the square root
> https://c-for-dummies.com/blog/?p=4250s

This Should Ring a Bell

```
#include <stdio.h>

int main()
{
        const int limit = 1000;
        int x;
        float t;

        /* divergent */
        t = 0.0;
        for(x=1; x<=limit; x++ )
                t += 1.0 / (float)x;
        printf("Divergent: %.4f\n", t);

        /* convergent */
        t = 0.0;
        for(x=1; x<=limit; x*=2 )
                t += 1.0 / (float)x;
        printf("Convergent: %.4f\n", t);

        return(0);
}
```

Guess the Output

Try to guess what the output is before moving to the next page.

The code calculates the sum of two types of harmonic series, divergent and convergent:

```
Divergent: 7.4855
Convergent: 1.9980
```

While these values may not seem frightening, the math behind them is considered terrifying to some.

Discussion

Like the Fibonacci sequence (refer to Chapter 21), a harmonic sequence consists of the sum of values. But for a harmonic series, these are a series of fractions that follow a pattern. When all the fractions are added together, they either diverge and increase in value, or they converge by getting closer to a specific value.

The first loop in the sample code represents a divergent harmonic series. It's the sum of values 1/1, 1/2, 1/3, 1/4, and so on up to 1/1000 in the code. The mathematical hieroglyphics for this type of series are shown in this figure:

$$\sum_{n=1}^{\infty} \frac{1}{n} = 1 + \frac{1}{2} + \frac{1}{3} + \frac{1}{4} + \frac{1}{5} + \frac{1}{6} + \frac{1}{7} + \cdots$$

A for loop uses variable x for the denominator values. Variable t calculates the sum. The n value is 1,000, set by constant limit. The expression t += 1.0 / (float) x represents the fractions shown in the previous figure. (Remember that one is also 1/1.)

The second loop represents a convergent harmonic series. Rather than increment by one, each fraction is a multiple of two, illustrated here:

$$\sum_{n=1}^{\infty} \frac{1}{n} = 1 + \frac{1}{2} + \frac{1}{4} + \frac{1}{8} + \frac{1}{16} + \cdots$$

In the code, the for loop calculating the convergent harmonic series uses the expression x*=2 to represent the values 2, 4, 8, 16, and so on.

To test how a harmonic series diverges or converges, increase the value of t in the code. For example, setting it equal to 1000000 (one million) generates this updated output:

```
Divergent: 14.3574
Convergent: 2.0000
```

The divergent value increases, though the new fractions added are smaller and smaller. But the convergent series homes in on the value 2. Weird, yes. But that's math—and one of the reasons mathematicians enjoy their science.

Further Reading

Details and other fun regarding harmonic series
https://study.com/learn/lesson/harmonic-series-formula-examples-what-is-a-harmonic-series.html

The harmonic series in music
https://www.oberton.org/en/overtone-singing/harmonic-series/

Harmonic series explained by Numberphile
https://www.youtube.com/watch?v=Jwtn5_d2YCs

More Math, but Fun This Time

```c
#include <stdio.h>

double phi(double p, int precision)
{
        while(precision)
                return( p + 1/phi(p, precision-1) );
        return(p);
}

int main()
{
        double gr;

        gr = phi(1.0, 15);
        printf("Phi is %f\n", gr);

        return(0);
}
```

Guess the Output

Try to guess what the output is before moving to the next page.

The code outputs the following line:

`Phi is 1.618034`

This is the golden ratio, represented by Greek letter phi, ϕ.

Discussion

The golden ratio is yet another of those mathematical joys that, like the Fibonacci sequence, appear frequently in nature. It's important enough to have its own Greek letter assigned, phi or ϕ.

Phi is a concept that's best illustrated as opposed to being explained in text. The diagram below illustrates how the ratio applies to two lengths, A and B.

In this diagram, ϕ is the ratio of line segment AB to line segment BC. Line segment ab is equal in length to line segment BC. And when compared with line segment AB, ab and bc are the same ratio as AB and BC.

Or something like that.

Math nerds, Mentats, and Vulcans use the following expression to describe the relationship between A and B illustrated previously:

`(AB+BC)/AB == AB/BC == ` ϕ

They also use this frightening equation:

`(1+?5)/2 = 1.6180339887...`

Like π, ϕ is an irrational number, which means that it cannot be expressed as the ratio of two integers. In fact, the written form for the ϕ calculation uses continued fraction hieroglyphics, illustrated here:

$$\Phi = 1 + \cfrac{1}{1 + \cfrac{1}{1 + \cfrac{1}{1 + \ddots}}}$$

It's this continued fraction that I use for this chapter's code. Like calculating π (refer to Chapter 22), the continued fraction begs for a recursive function such as phi() used in the code.

The phi() function is passed two values, p and precision. The precision value is the trigger that halts recursion, which relates to the precision, or accuracy, of the result. The continued fraction is represented by the return value:

```
p + 1/phi(p, precision-1)
```

This expression has an additional modicum of insanity in that 1 is really the only value tossed around. But it's what happens to that value that results in the final number, the golden ratio, or ϕ

Further Reading

Explore the golden ratio, the "divine proportion"
https://www.britannica.com/science/golden-ratio

Phi as it relates to other things, including Fibonacci numbers
https://r-knott.surrey.ac.uk/Fibonacci/phi.html

Numberphile on the golden ratio
https://www.youtube.com/watch?v=sj8Sg8qnjOg

Index

Thank you!

We hope you enjoyed this book and that you're already thinking about what you want to learn next. To help make that decision easier, we're offering you this gift.

Head on over to https://pragprog.com right now, and use the coupon code BUYANOTHER2024 to save 30% on your next ebook. Offer is void where prohibited or restricted. This offer does not apply to any edition of *The Pragmatic Programmer* ebook.

And if you'd like to share your own expertise with the world, why not propose a writing idea to us? After all, many of our best authors started off as our readers, just like you. With up to a 50% royalty, world-class editorial services, and a name you trust, there's nothing to lose. Visit https://pragprog.com/become-an-author/ today to learn more and to get started.

Thank you for your continued support. We hope to hear from you again soon!

The Pragmatic Bookshelf

SAVE 30%!
Use coupon code
BUYANOTHER2024

Rust Brain Teasers

The Rust programming language is consistent and does its best to avoid surprising the programmer. Like all languages, though, Rust still has its quirks. But these quirks present a teaching opportunity. In this book, you'll work through a series of brain teasers that will challenge your understanding of Rust. By understanding the gaps in your knowledge, you can become better at what you do and avoid mistakes. Many of the teasers in this book come from the author's own experience creating software. Others derive from commonly asked questions in the Rust community. Regardless of their origin, these brain teasers are fun, and let's face it: who doesn't love a good puzzle, right?

Herbert Wolverson
(138 pages) ISBN: 9781680509175. $18.95
https://pragprog.com/book/hwrustbrain

Pandas Brain Teasers

This book contains 25 short programs that will challenge your understanding of Pandas. Like any big project, the Pandas developers had to make some design decisions that at times seem surprising. This book uses those quirks as a teaching opportunity. By understanding the gaps in your knowledge, you'll become better at what you do. Some of the teasers are from the author's experience shipping bugs to production, and some from others doing the same. Teasers and puzzles are fun, and learning how to solve them can teach you to avoid programming mistakes and maybe even impress your colleagues and future employers.

Miki Tebeka
(110 pages) ISBN: 9781680509014. $18.95
https://pragprog.com/book/d-pandas

Numerical Brain Teasers

Challenge your brain with math! Using nothing more than basic arithmetic and logic, you'll be thrilled as answers slot into place. Whether purely for fun or to test your knowledge, you'll sharpen your problem-solving skills and flex your mental muscles. All you need is logical thought, a little patience, and a clear mind. There are no gotchas here. These puzzles are the perfect introduction to or refresher for math concepts you may have only just learned or long since forgotten. Get ready to have more fun with numbers than you've ever had before.

Erica Sadun

(186 pages) ISBN: 9781680509748. $18.95

https://pragprog.com/book/esbrain

Go Brain Teasers

This book contains 25 short programs that will challenge your understanding of Go. Like any big project, the Go developers had to make some design decisions that at times seem surprising. This book uses those quirks as a teaching opportunity. By understanding the gaps in your knowledge, you'll become better at what you do. Some of the teasers are from the author's experience shipping bugs to production, and some from others doing the same. Teasers and puzzles are fun, and learning how to solve them can teach you to avoid programming mistakes and maybe even impress your colleagues and future employers.

Miki Tebeka

(110 pages) ISBN: 9781680508994. $18.95

https://pragprog.com/book/d-gobrain

Agile Retrospectives, Second Edition

In an uncertain and complex world, learning is more important than ever before. In fact, it can be a competitive advantage. Teams and organizations that learn rapidly deliver greater customer value faster and more reliably. Furthermore, those teams are more engaged, more productive, and more satisfied. The most effective way to enable teams to learn is by holding regular retrospectives. Unfortunately, many teams only get shallow results from their retrospectives. This book is filled with practical advice, techniques, and real-life examples that will take retrospectives to the next level—whether your team is co-located, hybrid, or remote. This book will help team leads, scrum masters, and coaches engage their teams to learn, improve, and deliver greater results.

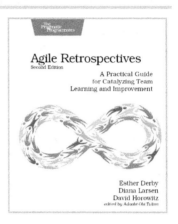

Esther Derby, Diana Larsen, David Horowitz
(298 pages) ISBN: 9798888650370. $53.95
https://pragprog.com/book/dlret2

Competing with Unicorns

Today's tech unicorns develop software differently. They've developed a way of working that lets them scale like an enterprise while working like a startup. These techniques can be learned. This book takes you behind the scenes and shows you how companies like Google, Facebook, and Spotify do it. Leverage their insights, so your teams can work better together, ship higher-quality product faster, innovate more quickly, and compete with the unicorns.

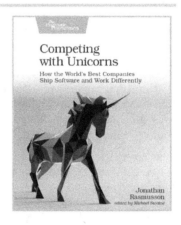

Jonathan Rasmusson
(138 pages) ISBN: 9781680507232. $26.95
https://pragprog.com/book/jragile

The Agile Samurai

Here are three simple truths about software development:

1. You can't gather all the requirements up front. 2. The requirements you do gather will change. 3. There is always more to do than time and money will allow

Those are the facts of life. But you can deal with those facts (and more) by becoming a fierce software-delivery professional, capable of dispatching the most dire of software projects and the toughest delivery schedules with ease and grace.

Jonathan Rasmusson
(264 pages) ISBN: 9781934356586. $34.95
https://pragprog.com/book/jtrap

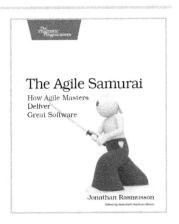

Driving Technical Change

If you work with people, you need this book. Learn to read co-workers' and users' *patterns of resistance* and dismantle their objections. With these techniques and strategies you can master the art of evangelizing and help your organization adopt your solutions.

Terrence Ryan
(146 pages) ISBN: 9781934356609. $32.95
https://pragprog.com/book/trevan

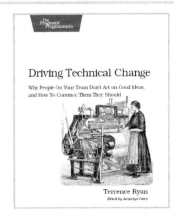

The Pragmatic Bookshelf

The Pragmatic Bookshelf features books written by professional developers for professional developers. The titles continue the well-known Pragmatic Programmer style and continue to garner awards and rave reviews. As development gets more and more difficult, the Pragmatic Programmers will be there with more titles and products to help you stay on top of your game.

Visit Us Online

This Book's Home Page
https://pragprog.com/book/cbrain
Source code from this book, errata, and other resources. Come give us feedback, too!

Keep Up-to-Date
https://pragprog.com
Join our announcement mailing list (low volume) or follow us on Twitter @pragprog for new titles, sales, coupons, hot tips, and more.

New and Noteworthy
https://pragprog.com/news
Check out the latest Pragmatic developments, new titles, and other offerings.

Save on the ebook

Save on the ebook versions of this title. Owning the paper version of this book entitles you to purchase the electronic versions at a terrific discount.

PDFs are great for carrying around on your laptop—they are hyperlinked, have color, and are fully searchable. Most titles are also available for the iPhone and iPod touch, Amazon Kindle, and other popular e-book readers.

Send a copy of your receipt to support@pragprog.com and we'll provide you with a discount coupon.

Contact Us

Online Orders:	*https://pragprog.com/catalog*
Customer Service:	*support@pragprog.com*
International Rights:	*translations@pragprog.com*
Academic Use:	*academic@pragprog.com*
Write for Us:	*http://write-for-us.pragprog.com*